12 SUPER-DANGEROUS ANIMALS
YOU NEED TO KNOW

by Jody Jensen Shaffer

12 STORY LIBRARY

www.12StoryLibrary.com

12-Story Library is an imprint of Peterson Publishing Company and Press Room Editions.

Produced for 12-Story Library by Red Line Editorial

Photographs ©: Michal Ninger/Shutterstock Images, cover, 1, 26; Raffaella Calzoni/Shutterstock Images, 4; Dennis Heidrich/iStockphoto, 5; Craig Dingle/iStockphoto, 6; Johan Larson/Shutterstock Images, 7, 28; cdelacy/iStockphoto, 8; Sergey Uryadnikov/Shutterstock Images, 9; Photos By Andy/Shutterstock Images, 10; Scott E. Read/Shutterstock Images, 11, 29; Mari Swanepoel/Shutterstock Images, 12; Martin Maritz/Shutterstock Images, 13; Gualtiero Boffi/Shutterstock Images, 14; Richmatts/iStockphoto, 15; Emi/Shutterstock Images, 16; Kevin Lings/Shutterstock Images, 17; WLDavies/iStockphoto, 18; 2630ben/iStockphoto, 19; claffra/Shutterstock Images, 20; doug4537/iStockphoto, 21; twphotos/iStockphoto, 22; Dougfir/iStockphoto, 23; guentermanaus/Shutterstock Images, 24; alexeys/iStockphoto, 25; jamenpercy/iStockphoto, 27

ISBN
978-1-63235-136-4 (hardcover)
978-1-63235-178-4 (paperback)
978-1-62143-230-2 (hosted ebook)

Library of Congress Control Number: 2015934274

Printed in the United States of America
Mankato, MN
June, 2015

Go beyond the book. Get free, up-to-date content on this topic at 12StoryLibrary.com.

TABLE OF CONTENTS

AMERICAN ALLIGATOR HUNTS ITS NEXT MEAL

American alligators are the top predators of their habitats. They can weigh 500 pounds (227 kg) and reach up to 15 feet (4.6 m) in length. They are the largest reptiles in North America.

An alligator lies in wait for its meal. Only its eyes and snout provide any hint it is there. The alligator's body remains submerged in the calm swamp water. Up to 80 razor-sharp teeth are ready to bite and rip its food. Eventually the alligator will be rewarded when a thirsty boar trots to the riverbank for a drink.

An alligator captures its prey with a quick lunge from the swamp. Its strong jaws hold

the frantic creature. The force of an alligator bite is powerful. It has been measured at around 3,700 pounds (1,678 kg). This is enough power to lift a small truck. Finally, the gator pulls its prey down in the water until it drowns. An alligator may roll its victim in the water. This confuses or drowns it. It might shake the victim and shatter its spine.

Alligators are found mainly in Florida and Louisiana. Alligators are carnivores. They eat fish, snails, and frogs. They also eat birds and mammals. Alligators mate in early May. The female builds a nest of plants. In late June or early July, she lays 35 to 50 eggs. Near the end

An alligator's teeth fall out regularly and are replaced by new ones.

15

Number of deaths reported in the United States from 1948 to 2004 as a result of encounters with alligators.

- Alligators injured 376 people in the United States between 1948 and 2004.
- Alligator encounters with humans are increasing.
- Dogs and cats are sometimes the victims of alligator attacks.

of August, the young alligators make high-pitched noises. The mother uncovers the eggs for hatching.

Hatchlings are 6 to 8 inches (15 to 20 cm) long. If the alligator

SAVING ALLIGATORS

American alligators were once endangered and at risk of extinction. Now they are thriving. State and federal governments protect them. Their habitats are preserved. And demand for products made from alligators is decreasing.

nest at hatching is 82 to 86 degrees Fahrenheit (28 to 30°C), the hatchlings will be female. If the nest is 90 to 93 degrees Fahrenheit (32 to 34°C), the hatchlings will be male. If the nest is 86 to 90 degrees Fahrenheit (28 to 32°C), both male and female hatchlings will be born. Alligators can reproduce when they are 10 to 12 years old.

American alligators can live for 35 to 50 years.

CASSOWARIES KICK AWAY THREATS

The double-wattle cassowary looks like a prehistoric creature. This bird cannot fly, but it can jump up to 5 feet (1.5 m) high. It can also run up to 30 miles per hour (48 km/h). A cassowary's kick is powerful enough to knock a man down.

Cassowaries are native to New Guinea and Australia. They are the world's second-heaviest bird at 128 pounds (58 kg). Only the ostrich is heavier. Cassowaries prefer to eat fruit from trees or from the ground. But they will also eat vertebrates and invertebrates.

There are three species of cassowary. All three have a casque, or helmet, on top of their heads. The casque feels spongy inside

A cassowary has 4.7-inch (12-cm) long dagger-like claws on each foot.

The casque starts to grow when a cassowary is one to two years old.

7.2

Average length, in feet (2.2 m), of the cassowary's wingspan.

- Cassowaries have only five to six flight feathers on each side.
- Historically, they had no natural predators.
- They adapted to life without flight.
- The last person to be killed by a cassowary was in 1926. Many injuries have happened since.

but is covered with a thin layer of stronger material. No one knows for sure, but some believe cassowaries use their casques to protect their heads as they push through thick rainforest plants.

Cassowaries mate between June and October. The male makes the nest. The female lays up to eight green eggs in it. The male incubates the eggs for 50 days. He raises the chicks for the next nine months.

GREAT WHITE SHARKS SINK TEETH INTO PREY

Great white sharks are the largest predatory fish on Earth. Adults can weigh up to 5,000 pounds (2,268 kg). They can grow to be 20 feet (6.1 m) long. Great white sharks' mouths can be nearly 3 to 4 feet (0.91 to 1.2 m) wide.

The great white shark spots a sea lion. The shark swims toward its prey at up to 15 miles per hour (24 km/h). When the shark is directly below the sea lion, it whips its powerful tail. The tail propels the shark upward like a torpedo. The great white shark collides with

Great white sharks live in both cool and tropical coastal waters around the world.

the sea lion and sends it reeling through the air. The shark opens its massive jaws and bites its victim with dagger-sharp teeth. The sea lion goes limp.

Female great whites have litters of two to ten pups, after being pregnant for one year. Newborn sharks are more than 3 feet (0.91 m) long. They are independent the minute they are born. Neither parent raises the pups. Some great white sharks can live to be 40 years old.

Great whites prey on seals, dolphins, and sea turtles.

FINDING PREY

Great white sharks have an excellent sense of smell. This helps them easily find prey. They can detect one drop of blood in 25 gallons (95 L) of water. They can even sense tiny amounts of blood in the water up to 3 miles (5 km) away.

11

Amount, in tons (9,979 kg), of food eaten by a great white shark in one year.

- Scientists estimate that after a big meal, a great white can go three months without eating.
- Many of the scratches on sharks' noses are the result of prey fighting back.
- When sharks attack people, it is likely because the sharks think the people are seals, its normal prey.

GRIZZLY BEAR MOTHERS DEFEND THEIR YOUNG

Grizzly bears are a type of brown bear. They are top predators in their habitats. And they are excellent at defending their young.

A mother grizzly bear sniffs the air. She can smell trouble before she sees it. A cougar lurks behind a boulder. It is watching the bear cubs. But the grizzly is not going to let anything happen to her young. She digs her 4-inch (10-cm) long claws into the ground and takes off running. She weighs nearly 500 pounds (227 kg). But she is amazingly fast. She gouges the cougar with her claws. She rips at its leg with her teeth. She saves her cubs for one more day.

Grizzly bears live in western Canada and Alaska. They also live in Wyoming, Montana, and Idaho. They can take down elk and deer. But most of the time,

Mother grizzly bears protect their young for a few years.

grizzlies eat grass, berries, and seeds.

Grizzlies mate between May and July. Mothers give birth while they are hibernating. They raise the cubs for two to three years. Then the cubs go off to live on their own. Grizzlies can live 20 to 30 years.

800

Approximate weight, in pounds (363 kg), of an adult male grizzly.

- Grizzlies can stand between 5 and 8 feet (1.5 and 2.4 m) tall.
- They can run up to 30 miles per hour (48 km/h).
- When preparing for hibernation, grizzlies can gain more than 3.5 pounds (7.7 kg) each day.

Grizzlies make their homes in meadows, plains, and the arctic tundra.

HIPPOPOTAMUSES CHARGE PREDATORS

Hippopotamuses are massive mammals. They can grow to 15 feet (4.6 m) long and 5 feet (1.5 m) tall. They weigh as much as 8,000 pounds (3,629 kg). Still, some animals that share the hippo's habitat challenge these creatures.

It starts as a staring contest. Hippo versus lion. The mother hippo stands guard over her calf. The lion approaches. The hippo shows her 12-inch (30-cm) long tusks. The lion attacks anyway, trying to dig its claws into the mother hippo's back. But the hippo's hide is 2 inches (5 cm) thick in some places. The lion falls. Suddenly, the hippo charges and spears the lion with her teeth.

Hippos live in central and southern Africa. They live in the desert. Hippos are herbivores that eat plants and grass. They walk single-file around a path, grazing on

A hippo yawning is a warning for predator to stay away.

12

Hippos sometimes come on land to find food.

grass. They can eat 80 pounds (36 kg) each night.

Hippo calves are born in shallow water or on land. They can weigh up to 100 pounds (45 kg). Calves eat grass when they are approximately three weeks old. They drink their mother's milk for up to one year. Hippos can live up to 40 years in the wild.

16

Approximate number of hours each day hippos spend submerged in water.

- Hippos are good swimmers.
- They can hold their breath for up to five minutes.
- Their eyes and nostrils are on top of their heads, so they can see and breathe while in the water.

HIPPO SUNSCREEN

Hippos bask on the shoreline and produce an oily red substance. This made some people claim that hippos sweat blood. The liquid is actually a skin moistener and sunblock. It may also provide protection against germs.

HYENAS SCAVENGE FOR FOOD

Spotted hyenas are the largest of the three species of hyena. All hyenas look similar to dogs. But they are more closely related to cats.

Hyenas often hunt at night. They use their good hearing and excellent eyesight to find a wildebeest herd.

One hyena runs through the herd, making whooping and laughing sounds. The others separate an old wildebeest. It tries to get away, but the hyenas are fast. Their jaws are powerful. They rip the wildebeest's flesh while it runs. Soon the hyenas overtake the wildebeest. In the

Hyenas live up to 25 years in the wild.

morning, all that remains are its horns.

Hyenas live in Africa, Arabia, and India. They are found in savannas, grasslands, forests, and mountains. Hyenas are not picky about what they eat. They are predators and scavengers. Hyenas eat hippo calves and antelopes. They feast on zebras and gazelles. They also eat carrion. Hyenas can even digest the bones and skin of other animals.

Hyenas have litters of two to four cubs. Cubs nurse for one year or more. They begin to eat meat at approximately five months old. If a mother hyena goes on a hunt, other adults in her clan watch her cubs.

80

Approximate number of members in a hyena clan.

- Hyenas are very territorial.
- The den is where cubs are raised and hyenas meet.
- Female hyenas rule clans.

KOMODO DRAGONS LUNGE FOR PREY

Komodo dragons are the heaviest lizards in the world. Males can weigh 330 pounds (150 kg) and reach 10 feet (3 m) in length. Despite their size, these dragons are patient hunters.

The Komodo dragon lies motionless in the shadows. It waits there for its next meal. Hours pass. Finally a deer wanders down the trail. The Komodo lunges. It bites the deer's leg. Its teeth tear the deer's flesh. The deer pulls away and limps off. But already more than 50 strains of bacteria have infected its body. In a few days, the wound will spread and its skin will begin to rot. Then, the Komodo dragon will use its excellent sense of smell to find its kill and eat it.

Komodo dragons live on islands in Indonesia. They live in tropical forests and on beaches. They hunt wild boar, deer, and water buffalo.

Komodo dragons mate between May and August. The female lays approximately 30 eggs in September. She incubates the eggs for nine months. Hatchlings weigh less than 3.5 ounces (1 g). They are 16 inches (41 cm) long.

Indonesians call Komodo dragons "land crocodiles."

Komodo dragons can live to be 30 years old.

2.5

Approximate distance, in miles (4 km), from which Komodo dragons can smell prey.

- If prey is small, Komodo dragons swallow it whole.
- A Komodo dragon's saliva helps lubricate food as it goes down.
- After digesting its meal, a Komodo vomits teeth, hooves, hair, and horns.

ELASTIC STOMACH

Komodo dragons have elastic stomachs. They can eat up to 80 percent of their body weight in one meal. When they are threatened and need to make a quick escape, they can throw up the contents of their stomach. This makes them lighter and quicker.

LIONS STALK PREY FROM TALL GRASSES

Lions are big cats. They can be 6.5 feet (2 m) long and weigh up to 400 pounds (181 kg). Lions are mammals and carnivores.

Lions usually hunt when it is dark. But sometimes they will hunt during the day. The lions creep through the long grass. They keep their backs low and their senses alert.

If a wildebeest looks up, the lions melt into the ground, hidden. Then they creep silently, slowly, until they are no more than 100 feet (30 m) away. The lions then charge. With long, powerful strides, they cover the distance quickly. The lions slap the wildebeest's legs with their large paws. The wildebeest stumbles.

Lions stalk their prey before attacking.

15

Approximate number of lions in a pride.

- Lions are the only cats that live in groups, called prides.
- Prides are mostly made up of females, their cubs, and a few males.
- Females do most of the hunting.

The lions pounce and bite the wildebeest's neck. The pride shares the kill.

Lions live throughout sub-Saharan Africa. They are found in grasslands, scrub, and open woodlands. Lions bring down prey with their hooked claws and large canine teeth. They primarily eat antelope and wildebeest. They also eat crocodiles, pythons, hippopotamuses, and porcupines. They also steal kills from hyenas.

Female lions have litters of three to four cubs. Cubs begin hunting with their mothers when they are 11 months old. Lions can live up to 14 years.

Females raise the lion cubs.

9

MOSQUITOES SUCK BLOOD AND CARRY DISEASE

Mosquitoes are insects. They are also carnivores. And though they are less than 1 inch (2.5 cm) long, they kill more humans each year than all of the other animals in this book combined.

It is dusk. A female mosquito flies toward a group of people. As she gets close, she detects the temperatures of their bodies. She senses the carbon dioxide they give off. She recognizes the lactic acid in their sweat. She lands and inserts her proboscis. When she finds a blood vessel, she injects saliva. It contains a substance that keeps blood from clotting. Then she sucks her victim's blood.

Mosquitoes prey on birds and reptiles. They also seek out amphibians and mammals, including humans. Every year, the diseases mosquitoes carry kill more than 3 million people. Some of these diseases include malaria, yellow fever, and encephalitis.

Mosquito eggs hatch into worm-like larvae. In less than one week, the larvae grow into pupae. The pupae grow into adult mosquitoes. Female mosquitoes usually live for two to three weeks. Males live for less time.

Mosquitoes can pass along dangerous diseases.

3,500

Approximate number of mosquito species.

- Three species are mainly responsible for spreading disease.
- Only female mosquitoes suck blood. They need it to produce eggs.
- Mosquitoes carrying malaria kill 3 million people each year.

PICKY EATERS

Mosquitoes are picky eaters. They prefer men to women. They would rather bite adults than children. And they like larger people over smaller ones. Why? Researchers believe it is because larger people produce more heat. They give off more carbon dioxide and they provide more surface area to bite.

Mosquitoes hatch from eggs laid in water.

ORCAS' TEETH GRASP AND TEAR

Orcas, also called killer whales, are not whales at all. They are the largest members of the dolphin family. Orcas can grow to 32 feet (9.8 m) and weigh 6 tons (5,443 kg). That is almost as big as a school bus! Despite their size, orcas are fast swimmers, especially when it is mealtime.

The hungry pod is on the move. They spot a group of sea lions. The orcas click to communicate the location and size of their prey. They swim closer and circle the sea lions. The orcas can reach speeds of more than 35 miles per hour (56 km/h). They force the sea lions into smaller and smaller areas. Then they take turns biting and ramming their prey. Orcas use 3-inch (7.6-cm) long teeth to grasp and tear.

Orcas can live in the wild for up to 80 years.

Orcas live in oceans throughout the world.

3
Number of types of orcas.

- Resident orca pods usually stay in one area and tend to prefer fish to eat.
- Transient orca pods are more aggressive and hunt marine mammals together.
- Offshore orcas look similar to resident orcas, but have different calls than resident or transient orcas.

Orcas are most common in the Arctic Ocean and Antarctic Ocean. They also live off the west coast of the United States and Canada. They are at the top of their food chain. They eat walruses, sea elephants, turtles, penguins, and squid. They will even attack sperm whales and blue whales.

Orcas live in pods of up to 30 members. Females lead pods. A female gives birth every three to ten years. Her calf can weigh up to 400 pounds (181 kg). It can be 7 feet (2.1 m) long.

11

PIRANHAS GO ON FEEDING FRENZIES

Piranhas are medium-sized fish with sharp teeth. Although they are known for eating meat, piranhas are omnivores. They eat both meat and plants.

The piranha first senses splashing. It feels the change in water pressure. Sensors along its sides detect movement. A capybara is injured. The piranha notices blood. It is on the move. With razor-sharp, interlocking teeth, the piranha punctures the capybara's flesh. Then it rips at the capybara's legs. Suddenly hundreds of piranhas

Piranhas can grow new teeth when old ones have fallen out.

descend. Each one darts, tears, and eats. It is a feeding frenzy.

Piranhas live in the rivers, lakes, and streams of South America. They feed on plants, fish, birds, and reptiles. They also eat rodents and other small mammals. If piranhas are starved and large prey is available, many fish will feed at one time.

A female piranha lays several thousand eggs in the water near plants. A male swims past and fertilizes the eggs. In two to three days, young piranhas hatch. They swim to the bottom and hide among the plants until they grow bigger. Both parents guard their young.

3
Number of vocalizations piranhas make.

- Piranhas bark, or make quick calls, when staring down other fish.
- When fighting another fish, a piranha emits low growls.
- If a rival does not back down, a piranha will gnash its teeth and chase the rival.

DRY SEASON

When food is scarce, piranhas are more aggressive than usual. During dry seasons, water levels fall in piranhas' river homes. When they do, piranhas get trapped in still pools. They eat all the food available to them. Then they focus on anything that enters the water.

25

WOLVERINES SNIFF FOR FOOD

Wolverines look like small bears. They are covered in thick hair. But wolverines are actually the largest members of the weasel family. And they are relentless predators.

From the top of its boulder, the wolverine can smell everything, including the caribou below it. Normally the wolverine would go for smaller prey, such as a rabbit. Muscles tensed, the wolverine leaps. His long claws grasp the caribou's back. His sharp teeth slice the caribou's flesh. The wolverine is fierce. Eventually the caribou dies of its wounds. What the wolverine cannot eat right away, he will spray with musk and return to later.

Wolverines live in the mountains of Europe, Asia, and North America. They live near or above the timberline, where no trees grow. The ground is often covered in snow where they live.

Wolverines can climb trees using their sharp claws.

Wolverines have huge paws that allow them to walk on top of the snow.

Wolverines are omnivores. They eat plants and berries. They also eat carrion, rabbits, and rodents. They will take down weak caribou, elk, and deer. Wolverines will even dig into burrows and eat hibernating animals. They may travel 15 to 18 miles (24 to 29 km) each day in search of food. Female wolverines in North America usually have one to two kits. Wolverines live up to 12 years in the wild.

30
Approximate weight, in pounds (14 kg), of an adult male wolverine.

- Wolverines are 26 to 36 inches (66 to 91 cm) long. They have a bushy tail that is 5 to 10 inches (13 to 25 cm) long.
- Though smaller than other mammals in their habitat, wolverines are fierce competitors.
- Wolverines are known to try to steal kills, even from much larger animals.

THINK ABOUT IT

Wolverines do not hibernate in the winter. What adaptations allow them to survive the harsh conditions? Use information from these pages to make a list of the wolverine's adaptations.

27

FACT SHEET

- Adult alligators, great white sharks, grizzly bears, Komodo dragons, and orcas are all top predators. They do not have any natural enemies who prey on them. However, the young of these animals are preyed upon.

- Some animals are predators and prey. Hyenas prey on wildebeests. Lions prey on hyenas and wildebeests. Crocodiles prey on lions.

- Some animals are omnivores. They eat plant matter as well as meat. Piranhas, wolverines, cassowaries, and grizzly bears are omnivores.

- Hippos are herbivores. They eat only plant matter. Because of their size, hippos pose a threat to anyone who stands between them and the water or between them and their young.

- The biggest surprise of these super dangerous animals is the mosquito. The smallest species by far, the mosquito is more deadly than all of the other animals combined. Though they do not have long claws, dagger-sharp teeth, the heft of a hippo, or the speed of an orca, mosquitoes kill 3 million people a year from malaria. Tens of millions more are killed or injured by other mosquito-borne diseases.

GLOSSARY

carnivore
A meat eater.

carrion
The dead or decaying flesh of an animal.

fertilize
To make an egg, plant, or animal able to grow.

incubate
To sit on eggs and keep them warm until they hatch.

invertebrate
An animal without a backbone.

mammal
A warm-blooded animal with fur that gives birth to live young.

omnivore
One who eats both plants and animals.

predator
An animal that preys on others for food.

prey
An animal that is hunted or killed by another for food.

pride
A group of lions that forms a social unit.

proboscis
A tubular sucking mouth part.

scavenger
An animal that feeds on dead animals, dead plant matter, and trash.

vertebrate
An animal with a backbone.

wattle
A wattle is the fleshy skin that hangs from an animal's head or neck.

FOR MORE INFORMATION

Books

De La Bédoyère, Camilla. *Brutal Beasts.* Orlando, FL: Ripley Publishing, 2013.

Henry, Claire. *The World's Deadliest Animals.* New York: PowerKids Press, 2014.

Jenkins, Steve. *The Animal Book: A Collection of the Fastest, Fiercest, Toughest, Cleverest, Shyest—and Most Surprising—Animals on Earth.* Boston: Houghton Mifflin Harcourt, 2013.

Websites

National Geographic Kids: Deadly 60
www.ngkids.co.uk/did-you-know/WATCH-CBBCs-Steve-Backshall-Deadly-60-clips-and-interview#

San Diego Zoo: Cassowary
animals.sandiegozoo.org/animals/cassowary

Wildscreen Arkive: Komodo Dragon
www.arkive.org/komodo-dragon/varanus-komodoensis

INDEX

About the Author

Jody Jensen Shaffer is the author of 21 books of fiction and nonfiction for children. She also publishes poetry, stories, and articles in children's magazines. When she's not writing, Jody copyedits for children's publishers. She works from her home in Missouri.

READ MORE FROM 12-STORY LIBRARY

Every 12-Story Library book is available in many formats, including Amazon Kindle and Apple iBooks. For more information, visit your device's store or 12StoryLibrary.com.